COLLEGE GOATs

THE GREATEST OF ALL TIME

GOATs OF COLLEGE MEN'S BASKETBALL

BY WILL GRAVES

SportsZone

An Imprint of Abdo Publishing
abdobooks.com

abdobooks.com

Published by Abdo Publishing, a division of ABDO, PO Box 398166, Minneapolis, Minnesota 55439.

Printed in the United States of America, North Mankato, Minnesota.
102025
012026

Cover Photo: Jerry Wachter/Sports Imagery/Getty Images Sport Classic/Getty Images
Interior Photos: Bettmann/Getty Images, 5, 13, 34–35; Library of Congress/Corbis Historical/VCG/Getty Images, 6; Rich Clarkson/NCAA Photos/Getty Images, 9, 10, 16–17, 25, 37; Focus On Sport/Getty Images, 14, 22, 29; George Long/Sports Illustrated/Getty Images, 18; John D. Hanlon/Sports Illustrated Classic/Getty Images, 21; Manny Millan/Sports Illustrated Classic/Getty Images, 26; AP Images, 30; Wally McNamee/Corbis Historical/Getty Images, 33; Streeter Lecka/Getty Images Sport/Getty Images, 38; Andy Lyons/Getty Images Sport/Getty Images, 40–41; Dylan Buell/Getty Images Sport/Getty Images, 42

Editor: Dalton Rains
Series Designer: Kate Liestman

Library of Congress Control Number: 2025939135

Publisher's Cataloging-in-Publication Data

Names: Graves, Will, author.
Title: GOATS of college men's basketball / by Will Graves
Description: Minneapolis, Minnesota: Abdo Publishing, 2026 | Series: College GOATs: the greatest of all time | Includes online resources and index.
Identifiers: ISBN 9781098298333 (lib. bdg.) | ISBN 9798384932130 (ebook)
Subjects: LCSH: College sports--Juvenile literature. | Basketball--Juvenile literature. | Sports records--Juvenile literature. | College sports--Records--Juvenile literature.
Classification: DDC 796.32363--dc23

TABLE OF CONTENTS

TOM GOLA

A star from the moment he took the court at La Salle High School in Philadelphia, Pennsylvania, Tom Gola could have gone anywhere for college in 1951. Dozens of schools offered the talented 6-foot-7 guard-forward an athletic scholarship. Gola chose to stick close to home instead. The decision made Gola a legend at La Salle University. Over his three seasons, Gola turned the small school in northwestern Philadelphia into an unlikely powerhouse.

La Salle coach Ken Loeffler nicknamed Gola "Mr. All-Around." That's because Gola could do just about anything on the court. Fans would scream "Go, Gola! Go!" whenever he had his hands on the ball, which was pretty much all the time.

Gola was a gifted scorer. He averaged nearly 21 points per game during his four seasons with the Explorers. He was just as dominant at the other end of the floor. A tenacious defender and high energy rebounder, Gola's 2,201 career boards remained atop the National Collegiate Athletic Association (NCAA) record book 70 years after he graduated.

Even after college, Gola rarely strayed far from Philadelphia. He helped the Philadelphia Warriors win a National Basketball Association (NBA) title as a rookie in 1956. He later returned to La Salle University as head coach from 1968 to 1970. The team went 23–1 during Gola's first season and finished the year ranked No. 2 in the country.

Meanwhile, La Salle soared to new heights. As a freshman, Gola led the Explorers to the National Invitational Tournament (NIT) title and was named the NIT's Most Valuable Player. During his junior season Gola guided La Salle to the NCAA championship game. He led a second-half surge that carried La Salle to a 92–76 victory over Bradley University. Gola, who had 19 points and 19 rebounds in the championship, was named the tournament's Most Outstanding Player (MOP).

Tom Gola averaged 18.7 rebounds per game for his career.

In 1955–56, Bill Russell (6) scored a total of 597 points and grabbed 609 rebounds.

BILL RUSSELL

Growing up in Oakland, California, Bill Russell wasn't always a star basketball player. When he started high school, he was only 5 feet, 10 inches. He was cut from his high school team as a junior. But he kept working. He also grew to 6-foot-8 by the time he was a senior. Even with Russell's growth spurt, the University of San Francisco Dons were the only college program to offer the gangly center a scholarship. Russell repaid the Dons' faith in him by becoming one of the most dominant defensive players in college basketball history.

In Russell's era, freshmen weren't allowed to play on college varsity teams. By the time Russell debuted in 1953–54, he was 6 feet, 10 inches and weighed 215 pounds. The sophomore used his size, speed, and leaping ability to overwhelm opponents. The Dons took off with their star center at the helm. He blocked shots on defense and dunked the ball with ease on offense. In 1954–55, San Francisco went 28–1 during Russell's junior season, racing to an NCAA title game matchup against defending champion La Salle.

Squaring off with Explorers star Tom Gola, Russell put up 23 points and grabbed 25 rebounds. That lifted the Dons to an easy 77–63 win. Though he was still a raw offensive talent, Russell's 118 points over five tournament games that year set a new record.

Russell and the Dons looked even better the following season. San Francisco went a perfect 29–0 and became the third program in NCAA history to win back-to-back championships. Russell capped off his college career in style, scoring 43 points and setting a Final Four record with 50 rebounds over two games.

WILT CHAMBERLAIN

When 7-foot-1 Wilt Chamberlain arrived at Kansas, everyone had high expectations. It did not take long for "Wilt the Stilt" to surpass fans' hopes. Early in the 1955–56 season, Chamberlain and the Kansas freshman team took down the varsity squad in a scrimmage. Chamberlain scored 42 points as the first-year players cruised to victory over their more experienced teammates. Kansas head coach Phog Allen called his center "the greatest player in the world."

In 1956, the sophomore Chamberlain joined the varsity team. He quickly made his mark. In his first start, Chamberlain put up 52 points and grabbed 31 boards in a victory over Northwestern. Both totals were new school records.

Opponents struggled to stop Chamberlain. Some teams sent two, three, or even four players to defend him. Others would hold the ball on offense, hoping to drain the clock and limit the number of opportunities Chamberlain had to score. All that defensive attention

FAST FACT

The only thing Chamberlain couldn't do was lead the Jayhawks to a national title. He recorded 23 points and 14 rebounds in the 1957 title game. However, Kansas still fell to North Carolina in triple overtime. The Jayhawks didn't even make the tournament the following season. Back then, only conference champions got to compete, and the field was much smaller.

didn't stop Chamberlain, though. He averaged 29.9 points and 18.3 rebounds per game in his two seasons with the Jayhawks. Both set program records.

Wilt Chamberlain (13) scored 29.6 points per game in 1956–57.

Jerry Lucas (11) won the Associated Press Player of the Year Award in 1960–61 and 1961–62.

JERRY LUCAS

Jerry Lucas knew how to work hard. Growing up in Ohio, he sometimes put up 5,000 shots a day. All that practice paid off during his career at Ohio State. The 6-foot-8 center could score from all over the floor.

Lucas did not waste time making an impact on the Buckeyes. In 1959–60, he teamed up with fellow sophomore John Havlicek on the varsity squad. The two stars led Ohio State to the Big Ten championship and a spot in the NCAA Tournament.

The Buckeyes won their four tournament games by an average of 19.5 points. In the national championship game, Lucas recorded 16 points and 10 rebounds on the way to a 75–55 win over California. The Ohio State star was named tournament MOP.

In each of his three years with the Buckeyes, Lucas led the NCAA in field-goal percentage. More than 62 percent of his shots dropped through the net. The accurate shooting led to many wins. With Lucas in the lineup, Ohio State went 78–6.

FAST FACT

Lucas was a winner wherever he played. In 1960, he helped Team USA grab gold at the Olympics in Rome, Italy. He also won an NBA title with the New York Knicks in 1973. That made Lucas the first basketball player to win a high school state title, an NCAA title, an Olympic gold medal, and an NBA championship.

ELVIN HAYES

Elvin Hayes made history the moment he stepped onto the court at the University of Houston. In 1964, Hayes and teammate Don Chaney became the first Black players to compete for the Cougars. The burly center known as "The Big E" was just getting started.

The Cougars had enjoyed only limited success before Hayes arrived. But they became nearly unstoppable during his three years on the varsity squad. Thanks to a fadeaway jump shot that was almost impossible to defend, the 6-foot-9 forward helped make Houston a powerhouse.

In the 1966 NCAA Tournament, Houston reached the regional semifinals. A year later, the team advanced to the national semifinals for the first time. The historic run set the stage for Hayes's senior season and a game that changed college basketball forever.

On January 20, 1968, Hayes and the Cougars hosted mighty University of California, Los Angeles (UCLA) in the Astrodome. The matchup became known as "The Game of the Century." A crowd of more than 52,000 people crammed inside the stadium to watch Hayes square off against the Bruins' star center Lew Alcindor.

UCLA rolled into the matchup on a 47-game winning streak. However, Hayes was on a mission to prove that he could play with anyone. The Cougars' star did more than show he belonged. He outplayed one of the greatest players in basketball history. Hayes torched Alcindor and the Bruins, scoring 39 points and lifting Houston to a 71–69 victory.

While the Bruins earned a bit of revenge by beating Houston in the national semifinals later that year, Hayes undoubtedly had a place among the best of the best. He averaged 31.0 points and 17.2 rebounds during his career and earned national player of the year honors after his senior season.

Elvin Hayes averaged 36.8 points per game in 1967–68.

LEW ALCINDOR

Many great players have to deal with extra attention from defenses. Lew Alcindor had an even bigger challenge. After the 7-foot-2 center's sophomore season, the NCAA decided to make it harder for tall players to score. A new rule banned dunks. It wasn't enough to slow down Alcindor, though. He responded by focusing on his legendary "skyhook." Alcindor would place the ball in one hand,

Lew Alcindor (33) left UCLA with a total of 2,325 points and 1,367 rebounds.

raise his arm high in the air, and loft it into the hoop. The hook shot was nearly unstoppable.

Alcindor was already a star when he arrived at UCLA. Newspapers had praised his skills in high school. He quickly showed off his talents in college too. Alcindor started his college career on UCLA's freshman team. In an early-season scrimmage, he lifted the first-year players to an easy victory over the varsity squad. Alcindor moved up to UCLA's top team in 1966. With their skilled big man leading the way, the Bruins went on a record-setting tear.

Alcindor held himself to a high standard. He constantly looked for ways to improve, even after great performances. Alcindor scored 56 points in his first varsity game. Afterward, however, the hard-working star said his shooting was only average and his defense could have been better.

UCLA went 88–2 during Alcindor's three years with the varsity team. Each season ended the same way. Delighted fans watched the Bruins cut down the nets as NCAA champions, while Alcindor was named tournament MOP.

FAST FACT

Alcindor converted to Islam during his time at UCLA. Soon after moving to the NBA, He changed his name to Kareem Abdul-Jabbar. Abdul-Jabbar won six NBA titles during his 20-year pro career.

PETE MARAVICH

Sporting a shaggy hairdo and thick socks, Pete Maravich didn't exactly look like a star. Yet few players shone as brightly as Maravich during his days with Louisiana State University (LSU). The crafty guard known as "Pistol Pete" didn't want to just play basketball. He wanted to put on a show.

The 6-foot-5 Maravich was a master inventor. He loved to create different moves. From hook shots to funky layups, Maravich did it all. During his days playing for his father, LSU head coach Press Maravich, he could put the ball through the hoop better than anyone. The younger Maravich averaged an amazing 44.2 points per game in college. He topped 50 points 28 times. And he finished his career with 3,667 points. Those were just two of his many NCAA records. His numbers might have been even higher if the three-point line had been around.

Maravich wasn't just a scorer, though. He loved to pass the ball too. He wasn't afraid to wrap the ball behind his back or flick a pass between his legs to an open teammate.

Maravich showed he was the NCAA's best player and earned national player of the year honors. However, he never got a chance to show off his skills in the NCAA Tournament. The Tigers didn't make the field during Maravich's career. Although the guard led LSU to a second-place finish in the Southeastern Conference (SEC) as a senior, the NCAA Tournament still only included conference champions.

Pete Maravich scored 1,381 points during the 1969–70 season.

UCLA center Bill Walton (32) recorded a conference-leading 148 assists in 1973–74.

BILL WALTON

John Wooden coached many great players during UCLA's historic college hoops run. Bill Walton was one of the best. However, the 6-foot-11 center didn't fit the mold of the typical Bruins player.

The free-spirited Walton wore his red hair long. He sometimes clashed with Wooden, who believed in sticking to a strict set of rules. But one thing Walton and Wooden had in common was a fierce desire to win.

When Walton began playing for UCLA in 1971–72, the Bruins were in the middle of a historic tear. They had won five straight titles. Walton kept the run alive. His smooth footwork made him a nearly unstoppable scorer in the paint. And his long arms helped him gobble up rebounds and blocks.

Walton was also the ultimate team player. The fun really began when he looked to pass. Walton loved to fling long passes to streaking teammates for easy buckets. Wooden called his young star the best outlet passer he'd ever seen.

UCLA went 30–0 in each of Walton's first two seasons. He scored 24 points in the Bruins' 1972 championship win. A year later, he capped off his junior season with a near-perfect performance in the 1973 national title game. Walton made 21 of 22 shots for a game-high 44 points as the Bruins routed Memphis State. UCLA's title streak ended in 1974, so Walton ended his college career with two NCAA titles. He also collected three Naismith Trophies. These awards go to the nation's top college player. With those accomplishments, Walton secured a place among the best players in college basketball history.

DAVID THOMPSON

David Thompson didn't jump toward the basket when he went in for a layup. The North Carolina State (NC State) guard flew. With his 44-inch (1.1-m) vertical leap, Thompson seemed to hover in midair. It was easy to see why he was nicknamed "Skywalker."

Thompson arrived on campus in 1971. That was one year before the NCAA allowed freshmen to play on varsity teams. Dunking was still against the rules when he first took the court in 1972. That didn't stop him from getting as close to the rim as possible. Thompson and fellow NC State guard Monte Towe perfected the alley-oop. Towe would heave the ball toward the basket. Then Thompson would snatch it out of the air and drop it through the hoop.

Catching alley-oops wasn't Thompson's only talent. He was a gifted shooter who led the Atlantic Coast Conference (ACC) in scoring for three straight years. With Thompson and Towe directing the offense and 7-foot-2 center Tom Burleson patrolling the paint, NC State went on a dominant title run in 1974. Along the way, Thompson dropped 28 points in a Final Four matchup against

FAST FACT

Thompson got one chance to dunk while he was in college. During his final home game as a senior, Thompson took a long pass and slammed it through the net. He was called for a technical foul. But Thompson didn't care. NC State was on the way to an easy win, and the crowd roared its appreciation.

powerhouse UCLA. The Wolfpack ended the Bruins' long run atop the NCAA in double overtime. Then Thompson scored 21 points in a title-game victory over Marquette. The high-flying guard had arrived at the top.

David Thompson (44) averaged 26.0 points in 1973–74.

Forward Larry Bird averaged 30.3 points per game during his career at Indiana State.

LARRY BIRD

Larry Bird took a winding path to basketball greatness. After graduating from high school in 1974, he went to Indiana University. However, he couldn't afford to stay there. So he moved home, played for a junior college and Amateur Athletic Union team, and worked odd jobs. Bird finally landed at Indiana State in 1976.

It didn't take long for Bird to feel at home with the Sycamores. They had never even made the NCAA Tournament before Bird arrived. However, with the 6-foot-9 forward at the helm, Indiana State became a household name. Bird wasn't very quick, and he couldn't jump very high, but that didn't matter. He was a wizard on the court.

Bird led the Sycamores to an 81–13 record during his three seasons. Bird was a gifted scorer. However, it was his passing that set Indiana State apart. In a matchup against Bradley University, Bird was double-teamed the entire game. All the attention left teammates wide open. Bird took only two shots all game. The Sycamores won anyway.

Bird and Indiana State really took off during his senior year. The Sycamores went undefeated in the 1978–79 regular season. Then Bird led them to the Final Four. The crafty forward posted 35 points, 16 rebounds, and nine assists in a win over DePaul.

A showdown with Michigan State and star Magic Johnson awaited in the title game. The Sycamores fell to the Spartans, but more than 35 million tuned in to watch the first showdown between two iconic players. March Madness became more popular than ever.

MAGIC JOHNSON

On many basketball teams, point guards are among the smallest players on the roster. That was not the case for the Michigan State Spartans. At 6 feet, 9 inches, Earvin "Magic" Johnson had the body of a power forward. However, he didn't play like one. He didn't move like one, either. Instead, Johnson's ball-handling skills and remarkable vision made him an unstoppable point guard.

Johnson had gone to high school a few miles away from the Spartans' arena in East Lansing, Michigan. In college, even more eyes focused on the local star. He thrived on the bigger stage. Before Johnson arrived in 1977, Michigan State's basketball program had played in the NCAA Tournament only twice. Now, with Johnson's electrifying passing leading the way, the Spartans made the tournament two seasons in a row.

As a sophomore in 1978–79, Johnson led Michigan State to its greatest season yet. The Spartans captured the Big Ten Conference title and then breezed to the NCAA title game against Indiana State and Larry Bird. In front of a huge TV audience, Johnson scored 24 points to take down the Sycamores. The Spartans celebrated their first national title.

FAST FACT

Michigan State players always had to be ready for a pass from Johnson. Some teammates found that out the hard way. Occasionally, an unexpected pass would slam into a player's face, leading to a nosebleed or two.

Magic Johnson (33) lifted Michigan State to a 75–64 victory in the 1979 NCAA National Championship.

Ralph Sampson (50) recorded 2,228 points and 1,511 rebounds in his four years with Virginia.

RALPH SAMPSON

Virginia coach Terry Holland tried to keep expectations low when the Cavaliers signed the 7-foot-4 Ralph Sampson. Holland told fans they shouldn't expect the incoming center to block every shot, grab every rebound, and score every time he touched the ball. No warning could lessen the excitement, though. Virginia fans welcomed Sampson in 1979 with open arms. Before Sampson had even played a game for the Cavaliers, a fan painted the words "Ralph's House" on top of the roof of the college's basketball arena.

Sampson certainly looked at home during his four seasons at Virginia. He combined the size of a center with the speed of a guard. Sampson could power his way to the basket for dunks and layups, but he was just as comfortable stepping away to take jump shots. That combination made him a nightmare matchup for opponents. Some coaches joked that the only way to stop Sampson was to hope he injured himself on his way to the game.

Unfortunately for Virginia opponents, Sampson rarely missed a game. Instead, he spent four years lifting Virginia to new heights. Sampson led the team to an NIT championship as a freshman. The following year, the Cavaliers grabbed a top seed in the NCAA Tournament. In the Elite Eight, Sampson piled up 22 points and 12 rebounds in a victory over Brigham Young University. The center had carried Virginia to its first ever Final Four appearance. By the end of his career, Sampson joined UCLA-great Bill Walton, becoming only the second player to win three Naismith Trophies.

MICHAEL JORDAN

Starting in the early 1970s, freshmen were allowed to play varsity. That meant first-year guard Michael Jordan got to play in the 1982 national championship. His North Carolina Tar Heels were trailing Georgetown by one point with less than a minute to go. Then he got his hands on the ball. Jordan pulled up and let it fly. He didn't even wait around for the ball to fall. He didn't have to. The ball splashed through the net to put the Tar Heels ahead for good.

The shot was the first of many incredible moments for Jordan. One thing that set him apart was that he always worked to improve. After his sophomore year, Jordan asked Coach Dean Smith how he could get better. Smith replied with a letter outlining eight things Jordan could do to become a better all-around player.

Jordan checked every box as a junior. He set career highs in assists and blocks per game. And he led his conference in scoring. By 1984, he was off to an NBA career that included six championships while playing for the Chicago Bulls. Many people have called him the best player of all time. And it all started with a jump shot on college basketball's biggest stage.

FAST FACT

Jordan wasn't always the best player on the court. During his sophomore year of high school, he failed to make the varsity team. Jordan had to play on the junior varsity team instead. A growth spurt between his sophomore and junior years helped lift him to the next level.

North Carolina guard Michael Jordan averaged 17.7 points per game in college.

In 1983–84, Hakeem Olajuwon led the NCAA in rebounds and blocks.

HAKEEM OLAJUWON

Growing up in Nigeria, Hakeem Olajuwon's first love was soccer. He didn't start playing basketball until he was 15 years old. When he came to the United States a few years later, he was 7 feet tall. But he weighed just 190 pounds. A steady diet of steak, candy, and ice cream helped Olajuwon bulk up for college basketball.

Those meals helped Olajuwon's body grow, but he was still hungry to prove himself on the court. The center debuted with Houston in 1981. During his three seasons with the Cougars, Olajuwon became the leader of the team. Houston loved nothing more than running the floor and slamming the ball through the basket.

When Olajuwon wasn't scoring, he was swatting away shots or gobbling up rebounds at the other end of the court. He averaged more than five blocks per game during his sophomore and junior seasons. During his senior year, the center's 207 blocks tied the NCAA single-season record.

The player known as Hakeem "The Dream" gave other teams nightmares. Even though he was a latecomer to the game, basketball came easy to Olajuwon. He soon grew comfortable knocking down jump shots farther from the basket.

The only thing Olajuwon didn't grab during his college career was a national title. Houston made the Final Four in each of Olajuwon's three seasons. The Cougars won two national semifinals. However, they never won a championship.

PATRICK EWING

Before Patrick Ewing came along in 1981, Georgetown was better known for churning out future politicians and judges than basketball players. Ewing changed that in a big way. He was such a sought-after player coming out of high school that more than 150 members of the media showed up to hear him commit to the Hoyas. The 7-foot center's decision put Georgetown on the basketball map.

Ewing's toughness and grit made a big impact on the court. Throughout his college career, he served as the Hoyas' defensive anchor. Opponents would drive into the lane only to have their shots swallowed up by No. 33's 8-foot wingspan. In each of his four college seasons, Ewing led the Big East in blocks. He became so dominant that one opposing coach said he'd consider calling in sick so he didn't have to watch his team lose to the Hoyas again.

Georgetown rarely lost during Ewing's run with the program. The Hoyas reached the national title game in 1982 before falling in a heartbreaker to North Carolina. However, Ewing led the team back to the championship game two years later. This time, the Hoyas and their superstar would not be denied. Georgetown powered past mighty Houston in the final. Ewing hadn't just put the Hoyas on the map. He propelled them to the top.

Patrick Ewing averaged 9.2 rebounds per game in college.

DANNY MANNING

In the spring of 1987, Danny Manning had to make a decision. If the 6-foot-10 forward chose to go pro, he was sure to be one of the top picks in the NBA Draft. Instead, he opted to play one more season with the Kansas Jayhawks.

Manning wanted another chance to play alongside good friend Archie Marshall, who had missed most of the previous season with a knee injury. Things didn't go as planned. Marshall injured his knee again early in the 1987–88 season. Manning and the Jayhawks limped into the NCAA Tournament with a so-so record of 18–11.

Kansas wasn't expected to do much in the NCAA Tournament. Fans thought that the Jayhawks needed a miracle to make a deep run. That's exactly what the team got. When the tournament began, the group took off. Manning piled up 24 points in a tournament-opening win over Xavier. He kept getting better with each game. "Manning and the Miracles" reached the Final Four, where they stunned Duke. Manning put up 25 points and 10 rebounds in the win.

A matchup against Oklahoma awaited in the title game. Kansas' conference rival had won in the teams' first two meetings that season. This time, the Jayhawks believed they could take down the Sooners. Coach Larry Brown told his players to keep it close, and Manning would find a way to win it in the end.

Brown was right. Manning scored four points in the final 14 seconds of the game. The ball ended up in the loyal star's hands as time expired. Manning left Kansas as a national champion.

Danny Manning recorded 31 points and 18 rebounds in the 1988 title game.

CHRISTIAN LAETTNER

Christian Laettner, a 6-foot-11 center, had made Duke a polarizing team. Many were eager to see the defending national champion Blue Devils lose to Kentucky in the 1992 Elite Eight. With 2.1 seconds remaining in overtime, the Wildcats led by a point. Duke needed to go the length of the floor and score if it wanted to keep its hopes of a second straight national title alive.

Coach Mike Krzyzewski drew up a play during a timeout. He asked forward Grant Hill to throw a long pass to Laettner. Coach K didn't need to ask if Laettner could make the shot. The forward had already attempted 10 free throws and nine field goals. He'd made all 19 shots.

Hill tossed a 75-foot (23-m) dagger to an open Laettner near the Duke free-throw line. Laettner caught the pass, faked to his left, dribbled once to his right, and then turned around and let it fly. The final buzzer sounded as the ball splashed through the net. Laettner's 20th basket of the game locked down a Duke victory.

Two games later, the Blue Devils won the national title again. It never would have happened without The Shot. Laettner's efforts

FAST FACT

Laettner's charmed year continued in the summer of 1992. He was the only college player to play on the United States' gold-medal winning Olympic men's basketball team. Laettner joined NBA superstars Michael Jordan, Magic Johnson, and Larry Bird on "The Dream Team."

throughout the 1991–92 season earned him a Naismith Trophy. He left Duke with a career average of 16.6 points and 7.8 total rebounds per game.

Christian Laettner (32) played a total of 23 NCAA Tournament games with Duke.

Tyler Hansbrough piled up 2,872 career points. That set a conference record.

TYLER HANSBROUGH

No one played harder than Tyler Hansbrough during his stint at North Carolina in the late 2000s. The 6-foot-9 forward was called "Psycho T" for his relentless style of play. Hansbrough drew his strength from his older brother, Greg. Although Greg was partially paralyzed as a child, the elder Hansbrough brother overcame the diagnosis and was able to play sports. Greg wore the No. 50 on his high school jersey. At North Carolina, Tyler wore the same number to honor his brother.

Hansbrough gave his best effort every time he took the court. That mindset led the forward to a record-setting career with the Tar Heels. He became the first player in North Carolina history to lead the team in points and rebounds for four straight seasons.

However, Hansbrough was focused on winning games, not setting records. As a junior, he was disappointed by a Final Four loss in the 2008 NCAA Tournament. So he turned down the chance to play in the NBA in order to stay one more season with the Tar Heels. Hansbrough was on a mission. North Carolina demolished its opponents on the way to the national championship game. After crushing Michigan State 89–72 to clinch the title, Hansbrough knew he'd made the right decision.

Hansbrough left college as one of the greatest Tar Heels of all time. He ended his career as North Carolina's leading scorer in NCAA Tournament play. North Carolina retired his jersey in 2010. No other Tar Heel would wear the No. 50.

ANTHONY DAVIS

Anthony Davis wasn't always the biggest player on the court. Growing up in Chicago, he had played point guard. That changed when a late growth spurt saw him sprout to 6 feet, 10 inches.

Although Davis's body changed, he kept his guard skills. All those years running the point helped make Davis one of the most coveted recruits in the country. Davis said that moving from guard to forward took some getting used to, but it hardly looked like it during his time at Kentucky.

By the time Davis arrived on campus in 2011, Kentucky had gone nearly 15 years without a championship. That seemed like a lifetime for one of the most decorated programs in the country. Everyone knew Davis was likely to leave for the NBA after his freshman season. The Wildcats had to make the season count. As the centerpiece of a talented team stuffed with future NBA players, Davis hoped to bring the Wildcats back to the top.

With Davis controlling the paint on both ends of the floor, Kentucky went unbeaten in SEC play and earned a No. 1 seed in the 2012 NCAA Tournament. Winning each of their games by at least eight points, the Wildcats stormed to the national championship. Facing Kansas for the NCAA title, Davis struggled to find his shot. However, he had no trouble on defense. The lanky forward tied an NCAA-championship record with six blocks. He also recorded 16 rebounds and five assists as the Wildcats snatched their first title since 1998.

Anthony Davis, *top*, averaged 14.2 points per game in 2011–12.

Zach Edey led the NCAA in scoring in 2023–24.

ZACH EDEY

Growing up in Canada, Zach Edey dreamed of becoming a professional hockey player. The young athlete's body had other plans. Edey was nearly 6 feet tall by the time he was eight. He soon outgrew hockey and moved on to baseball. It wasn't until he was a teenager and had grown to more than 7 feet tall that basketball became his focus.

The massive center was still a work in progress when he came to Purdue in 2020. He didn't become a starter until his sophomore year. The Boilermakers' basketball program was a work in progress too. Purdue regularly made the NCAA Tournament, but the team had not made it to the Final Four since 2000.

Edey blossomed during his junior season. He took an old-school approach to the game. His offense relied on smooth footwork and a soft touch around the basket. The 7-foot-4 star won back-to-back national Naismith Trophies in 2023 and 2024. As his skills developed, Edey became harder and harder to stop. Purdue became harder to stop too.

The Boilermakers reached the national championship game in 2024. Edey piled up 37 points, 10 rebounds, and two blocks in the final game of his college career. It wasn't enough to lift Purdue to a win. However, the performance proved that Edey could keep up with the best of the best.

HONORABLE MENTIONS

JERRY WEST

West was a high-scoring guard from the hills of West Virginia. Starting in the late 1950s, he averaged nearly 25 points a game in three seasons with the West Virginia Mountaineers.

OSCAR ROBERTSON

Robertson was a triple-double machine for Cincinnati in the late 1950s. The guard led the Bearcats to the Final Four in both 1959 and 1960.

BILL BRADLEY

Bradley made Princeton a basketball power in the 1960s. The forward averaged more than 30 points per game during his junior season and led the Tigers to the 1965 NCAA semifinals.

SHAQUILLE O'NEAL

Starting in 1989, the 7-foot-1 O'Neal spent three seasons at LSU tearing down baskets with his dunks and setting records with his blocks.

LARRY JOHNSON

The 6-foot-6 Larry Johnson's thunderous dunks and ferocious rebounding made him one of the most intimidating players in the country. In 1990, the power forward led the University of Nevada, Las Vegas (UNLV) to an NCAA title.

CHRIS WEBBER

Webber was the heart and soul of "The Fab Five." The forward led Michigan's young stars to NCAA title-game appearances in 1992 and 1993.

RICHARD HAMILTON

A crafty guard, Hamilton averaged nearly 20 points a game in three seasons with Connecticut. He lifted the Huskies to their first title in 1999.

CARMELO ANTHONY

Anthony spent just one season at Syracuse, but the 6-foot-8 forward was able to lead the Orange to an upset over Kansas in the 2003 NCAA championship game.

GLOSSARY

amateur

A person who plays a sport without getting paid.

assist

A pass that leads directly to a basket.

conference

A group of schools that join together to create a league for their sports teams.

converted

Changed religions.

paralyzed

Unable to move part or all of the body.

polarizing

Causing divided opinions.

recruit

An athlete whom a college team is interested in.

rival

An opponent with whom a player or team has a fierce and ongoing competition.

scholarship

Money awarded to a student to pay for education expenses.

varsity

A school's top team in a sport.

MORE INFORMATION

BOOKS

Clayton, David. *Basketball Legends*. Welbeck, 2024.

Mahoney, Brian. *GOATs of Basketball*. Abdo, 2022.

Monnig, Alex. *Basketball*. Abdo, 2023.

ONLINE RESOURCES

To learn more about the GOATs of college men's basketball, please visit **abdobooklinks.com** or scan this QR code. These links are routinely monitored and updated to provide the most current information available.

INDEX

ABOUT THE AUTHOR

Will Graves has worked for more than two decades as a sports journalist. Since 2011, he has served as correspondent for the Associated Press in Pittsburgh, Pennsylvania, where he covers the NHL, the NFL, MLB, and various Olympic sports.